FIND YOUR PURPOSE

A Practical Guide for Discovering Your Purpose and Creating a Life You Love

SARAH CHOY & GEORGE CHOY

FIND YOUR PURPOSE

Find Your Purpose: A Practical Guide for Discovering Your Purpose and Creating a Life You Love

First published in the United Kingdom on 1 June 2022
This v2 edition published 20 January 2023

© 2023 George David Choy & Sarah Jane Choy

George David Choy and Sarah Jane Choy have asserted their right to be identified as the authors of this work in accordance with sections 77 and 78 of the Copyright, Designs and Patents Act 1988.

All rights reserved. No part of this book may be reproduced by any means, electronic, mechanical, photocopying or otherwise, without the prior permission of the publisher.

British Library Cataloguing in Publication Data

A catalogue record is available for this book

Paperback ISBN: 9798831520545

My Castle Property Ltd
27 Abbott Way, Tenterden, Kent, TN30 7BZ, United Kingdom.

Disclaimer

This book is intended to provide general information about designing your life. It is not an advice book, and its contents are not tailored to your specific circumstances. In particular, the contents of this book do not constitute financial, medical or psychological advice and neither the authors nor My Castle Property Ltd are regulated financial advisors, medical physicians, or psychiatrists.

You must not rely on the information in this book or the accompanying materials available for download as an alternative to financial, investment, legal, psychological or medical advice from an appropriately qualified professional. You should never delay seeking professional advice because of the information contained in this report.

You should always seek the advice of your doctor, physician, or psychiatrist if you are or suspect you are suffering from depression or other mental illness.

No warranty is made with respect to the accuracy or completeness of the information contained herein or in the accompanying materials available for download, and both the authors and My Castle Property Ltd specifically disclaim any responsibility for liability, loss, or risk, personal or otherwise, which is incurred as a consequence, directly or indirectly of the use and application of any of the contents of this book or accompanying downloads.

This disclaimer will be governed by and construed in accordance with English law, and any disputes relating to this disclaimer will be subject to the exclusive jurisdiction of the courts of England and Wales.

About Sarah and George Choy

Sarah and George became financially free through property investing, when Sarah was only 39 years old. Together, they own a multi-million residential and commercial property empire, which they manage in a passive way, requiring very little work.

They live their dream life and purpose every day. In their spare time they mentor and teach people to achieve the same financial success and design their own dream life. They also publish a vlog with lots of inspiration and tips. They live in the UK, with their two kids and a cat.

Follow Sarah and George at linktr.ee/sarahandgeorge

Dedication

This book is dedicated to the millions of lost souls, confused about their purpose and how to live a happy life. We want to change that.

Our purpose is to live our dream life, and help our family and others to do the same.

We'd feel truly blessed and inspired to find out what purpose you've chosen, or any ah-ha moments you had while reading this book.

Sending you love,
Sarah and George

Contents

CHAPTER 1 .... **11**

INTRODUCTION TO THE JOURNEY 11
    The Law of Dharma (Purpose) 13
    The five phases of Purpose transition 15
    The Purpose Formula 17
    Download the Workbook 17

CHAPTER 2 .... **19**

LIFE CHALLENGES 19

CHAPTER 3 .... **23**

PASSIONS 23
    Reticular Activating System (RAS) 24

CHAPTER 4 .... **37**

YOUR GIFTS 37

CHAPTER 5 .... **41**

ENVIRONMENT 41
    Internal Environment 41
    Maslow's Hierarchy of Needs 45
    External Environment 48
    Change Your Environment 50
    Seasons of Purpose Model 51

CHAPTER 6 .... **55**

ULTIMATE LIFE VISION (ULV) 55
    Your Ultimate Life Vision 56
    Your Ultimate Self 58
    Appreciating the journey 59

CHAPTER 7 .... **63**

12-Month Goals 63

CHAPTER 8 67

Identity 67
   3-Step Identity Transition Protocol 68

CHAPTER 9 73

Your Driving Question 73

CHAPTER 10 79

The 6 Human Needs and Contribution 79
   1. Certainty 80
   2. Uncertainty/Variety 82
   3. Significance 83
   4. Love and Connection 85
   5. Growth 87
   6. Contribution 88
   How the 6 Human Needs Fit Together 89

CHAPTER 11 93

The Purpose Formula in Action 93
   Your Elements OF The Purpose Formula 93
   Take a Moment to Reflect 94
   Three Feet From Gold 94
   Environmental Changes 97
   Don't Deny Your Purpose 99
   Critical for Your Health 100
   Drifting 101
   Your Purpose Can Be Small 101
   Gandhi 103

CHAPTER 12 107

Finding and Getting Paid for Your Purpose 107
   The Purpose Poster 107
   Live Your True Life 108

INTRODUCTION TO THE JOURNEY

Get Paid for Your Purpose 109
Starting a Side Hustle 112
Conclusion 113
We'd Love To Hear From You 114

FIND YOUR PURPOSE

Introduction to the Journey

"It is in your moments of decision that your destiny is shaped."
— Tony Robbins

Thank you so much for buying this book.

No matter how lost you feel at the moment, I want you to know that you are a beautiful soul, and you are worthy of having your dream life.

I lived an unfulfilling life in the past. I've often had jobs I didn't enjoy, colleagues I disliked, and managers I didn't like working for.

If you've been anything like me, then at some time you may have thought "I hate my job, but I need the money."

Or, "I'm bored with my job, but I don't know what else to do."

"What am I doing with my life?"

"I think I'm experiencing burnout."

"I think I'm going through a mid-life crisis."

"I feel disconnected from the world. Like I'm in a void."

"On paper my life is great. But for some reason I feel unfulfilled and I don't know why."

"What's my purpose now? Why am I here?"

Or if you're feeling really depressed, "What's the point of living anymore."

I've learned through myself and others, that we don't have just one purpose on this planet. You may be destined for multiple purposes throughout your lifetime, as your environment changes.

I've lost and gained a new purpose multiple times in my life. That's not unusual, even for the most significant people of our time. I expect more to come — particularly as life expectancy continues to increase.

I wrote this book to help millions of people find their purpose — and also as a step-by-step manual for myself, my wife and my children. I've instructed Sarah to ask me to read it again, if she ever notices the symptoms in me. We'll cover the symptoms that you've lost your purpose later.

I've read a lot of books on finding your purpose and most of them are really woolly. They give big promises, but by the end of them, you're no clearer on your purpose than when you started.

So, I designed this book to be really practical, and take you by the hand, to your purpose in life.

As you step through the exercises in this book, you'll build a picture of your life and learn your programmed responses. You'll get to understand your passions, gifts, how situations impact you, and the drivers for every decision you've ever made.

You'll already be aware of some of these elements, but may never have looked at them holistically before. You'll discover other parts of yourself for the first time, and get an 'ah-ha' moment. Once we've built this picture of YOU, then we can identify the optimum Purpose for you that brings the most joy, the most happiness, and the most fulfilment.

You can find a way to get paid for it. You will be so awesome at it, that you can earn a substantial amount of money. However, I ask that as you read this book, don't think about the money at all. Just focus on your true life-Purpose, let go of the fruit, and the money will follow.

THE LAW OF DHARMA (PURPOSE)

The Bhagavad Gita is the most famous of Hindu texts on Dharma — written sometime between 400 BCE and 200 CE. It contains a dialogue between prince Arjuna and his guide Krishna (who is later revealed to be God).

The Gita was the book that shaped Mahatma Gandhi's life and purpose — more about him later. The Gita was a constant companion to him, particularly in his darkest hours.

"Dharma" comes from the Sanskrit root word dhri, which generally means to "preserve." In general terms, it represents the cosmic law which creates harmony in universe. All beings should accept their Dharma in order for harmony to be maintained.

Deepak Chopra reduces it beautifully, to an individual level:

> *"Everyone has a purpose in life... a unique gift or special talent to give to others. And when we blend this unique talent with service to others, we experience the ecstasy and exultation of our own spirit, which is the ultimate goal of all goals."*

Consequently, it is your sacred duty to find and live your Dharma — not only to bring you joy, but for the benefit of all beings and the universe.

INTRODUCTION TO THE JOURNEY

THE FIVE PHASES OF PURPOSE TRANSITION

In hindsight, there's been an obvious pattern every time I've lost and gained my new purpose.

THE FIVE PHASES OF PURPOSE TRANSITION

PHASE 2: DECISION
Decide to end your old purpose. Relief, illness improves.

PHASE 5: TRANSFORMATION
Enthusiastic about new purpose. Energised, fulfilled, happy.

PHASE 4: ACCEPTANCE
Accept your new purpose. Enthusiasm, health improves.

PHASE 1: CRISIS
Loss of hope, depression, something missing, frustration, confusion, illness.

PHASE 3: PROTECTION
Reluctant to release old purpose. Poor sleep, illness, confusion.

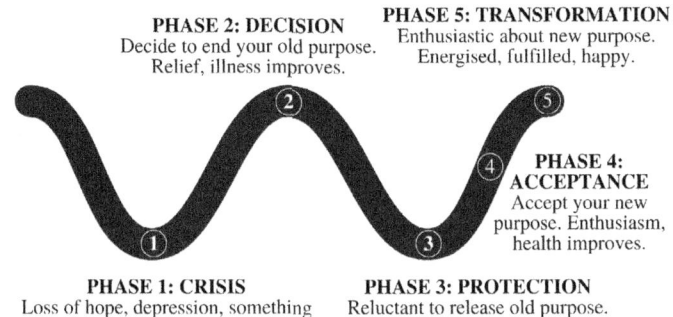

Phase 1: Crisis

It starts with loss of hope, depression, or the feeling that something is missing, or frustration with your life.

Warning signs — your subconscious mind may attempt to sabotage you from doing your current job, through headaches, migraines, depression, lack of energy and illness. Or if you have a physical job, then seemingly innocent accidents like twisting your ankle might happen. These symptoms may increase if you continue your current work.

I've met people who have frequent migraines. And after speaking with them for a while, it becomes very obvious that they are doing work they hate, and with people they dislike. Their mind is giving them a really strong signal to stop, but they feel they can't stop.

You need to allow these emotions to come to the surface. Acknowledge them. Talk about them with a loved one, or write down your feelings. It's important to get them out of you, as part of the healing process.

Phase 2: Decision
You go from feelings of confusion, to deciding to quit your current work or purpose. You'll feel an initial sense of relief. The moment you leave your job, the warning signs may either continue, or decrease and completely disappear.

Phase 3: Protection
Your conscious mind will wrap its hands around your old purpose and identity, and try to hold on it for dear life! Your mind believes it is what makes you, "you" — so it will not go without a struggle. You may become ill and have many nights of poor sleep. You'll feel confused until you find your new purpose, and move to the next stage.

Phase 4: Acceptance
When you've accepted your new purpose, you feel a huge sense of relief, and are enthusiastic about your new direction. Occasionally there are a few poor nights of sleep, but less frequent, and mainly due to exciting ideas you are having.

I've previously been sick for a month, while I was confused about my purpose. When I finally decided I would change my focus in the business and stop doing tasks I disliked, I miraculously recovered the following day. It's amazing how the mind not only has the power to heal the body, but also to make the body ill.

Phase 5: Transformation
You have a surge of energy and tireless enthusiasm about your new purpose. You lose track of time when you're doing it. Your life aligns around it. You feel fulfilled and happy. Amazing transformations appear.

THE PURPOSE FORMULA

I've developed a formula for finding your purpose. I'll go deep on it, as I guide you step-by-step through this book, to lead you to your most fulfilling purpose.

Passions x Gift(s) x Environment x Contribution = Purpose

DOWNLOAD THE WORKBOOK

I recommend you pause for a moment, to download the FREE workbook exercises and Purpose Poster at https://rebrand.ly/purposeworkbook

It will increase your likelihood of successfully finding your Purpose — which is what I want to bless you with.

We will get to the Purpose Poster towards the end of this book, so just save it for the moment.

FIND YOUR PURPOSE

CHAPTER 2

Life Challenges

"Challenges are gifts that force us to search for a new centre of gravity. Don't fight them. Just find a new way to stand."
— *Oprah Winfrey*

You'll experience multiple challenges as your life progresses. Some of these will be significantly more difficult than others, leading to a greater influence on your life's purpose. Frequently, they're a trauma, or something missing from your life — a void that you're trying to fill. You can think of them as a step on the way to something greater.

For example, when Arnold Schwarzenegger started building noticeable muscles, his school friends and teachers gave him more attention. Bodybuilding seemed to fill the void in his life:

"I'm not sure why I had this need for special attention. Perhaps it was because I had an older brother who'd received more than his share of attention from our

father.
Whatever the reason, I had a strong desire to be noticed, to be praised."
— *Arnold Schwarzenegger*

Tony Robbins had a poor childhood and suffered abuse. He often recounts one of the worst days of his life.

Tony heard a knock at the door and opened it. There stood a large man with a box of food and an uncooked turkey.

He interrupted his father screaming at his mother in another room and got him to come to the door. When his father saw the food, he raised his voice and said, "Look, we don't take charity."

His father tried to slam the door in the man's face — but the man put his foot in the gap.

The man said, "Sir, Sir. This is not charity. Everybody has tough times. Somebody knows you're having a tough time…don't make your family suffer because of your ego."

Tony's father took the food and slammed the door in the man's face. His father stormed off and went back to screaming at his mother. Shortly after that, his father left their family.

Tony recounts that as the most crushing and worst day of his life. However, he decided to give that day a new meaning. "If strangers care about me and my family. I decided what I was going to do, is I was going to care about strangers."

That experience led to him collaborate with Feeding America. Since 2015, he has provided over 860 million meals to people in need.

Here are some examples from my life that I'll refer back to later.

- I had a very poor childhood. I always felt that our family had a lot less money than everyone else. This made me feel like a third-class citizen for decades — even when I was earning a good salary.

- When I was at secondary school, I was short, overweight, and of course, looked Chinese. Therefore, it won't surprise you to know that I was frequently bullied.

- I went into a massive depression in my corporate job. I felt incredibly lonely from all the travelling, working long hours and weekends. I was also burned out from stress and office politics.

- When Sarah was 39 years old, we realised we were completely financially free, due to the income from the rental properties we owned. We never needed to work again. On paper our life was amazing — we did anything we wanted each day. However, for the first two years, we felt empty. We were unfulfilled. We hadn't realised that it was time to give, by living our true life-purpose.

- Sarah had a lot of difficulty getting pregnant. We suffered many years of disappointment and challenge.

Open the Find Your Purpose Workbook

If you haven't downloaded your free workbook and Purpose Poster yet, then get it at:
https://rebrand.ly/purposeworkbook
It will save you a lot of time.

Workbook Question 1. Write down a list of the most significant challenges you've experienced, starting from your childhood.

Please answer this question before reading further, as the exercises in this book will lead you to your Purpose by the time you finish this book.

Please don't answer any question until you've read the relevant chapter, otherwise your answers could be completely off track.

CHAPTER 3

Passions

"People with passion can change the world."
— Steve Jobs

Passions are the first variable we'll cover in the "Purpose Formula," as that's what most people think of, when they wonder what their purpose is.

Passions are those activities you feel are the most fulfilling, inspiring and interesting.

Perhaps you completely lose track of time when you're doing them. You could spend many hours on them and rarely get tired.

There may also be activities that make you feel like you are "in flow" or "in the zone." It's almost as if the entire world has disappeared, and you've put your entire focus on this one single moment.

Sometimes these Passions stem from one of your Life Challenges — which is why I asked you to write a list of them in the previous chapter.

Reticular Activating System (RAS)

Your brain processes around 11 million bits of information per second. That's such an overwhelming amount of data, that we could be paralysed if we consciously tried to comprehend it in one go.

Therefore, nature cleverly developed the Reticular Activating System, to help us cope with life. The RAS is the part of your brain which connects your subconscious mind, to your conscious mind. It helps you to function, by filtering life according to what you feel is important, interesting, or your beliefs. Your beliefs may be good — or they may be completely irrational and untrue. It's how you view the world.

Your RAS will distort, delete, and generalise how you perceive the world. It will draw your attention to people, adverts, news, places, events, ideas and anything it can find, that it thinks are useful.

You literally create your own reality, unique to you, and have the power to change it.

So, if you and I were experiencing the exact same moment together, we would perceive it very differently.

For example, have you ever decided to buy, or recently bought a car, and now you see it everywhere? It seems to be every third or fourth car you see when you're driving. You see adverts for it. You notice it in the news and on social media. Did everyone start buying that car? No, it's your RAS finding them.

Another example is when you hear your name spoken quietly on the other side of a noisy room. You're RAS zooms in on it.

When Sarah and I were trying for a baby, suddenly we saw pregnant women and children in buggies everywhere. Were more people having babies this year? No, it was just our RAS drawing attention to them.

Now, of course the RAS can also do this negatively — it does not discriminate. If you constantly have negative thoughts like, "I don't have any money," "I'm not good enough," "I'm fat," or "Why do all these bad things keep happening to me," then your RAS will seek out data to prove that you are right.

But the good news is that YOU have the power to change your thoughts…and change your reality.

Instead, start to feel gratitude when you do receive money, when you do release body fat, when good things do happen to you — your life will change positively.

*****

PASSIONS RELATED TO LIFE CHALLENGES

After reviewing the Life Challenges you wrote down in question 1, you might notice some that some of your Passions are related to them.

For example, perhaps you experienced poverty as a child and now you read, watch and listen to everything you can find about making money — you also take a lot of action on it too. That happened to me. I have a very strong passion for financial freedom and financial security due to my poor upbringing, and due to the time when Sarah and I could barely afford to buy food to eat.

Another great example is Pete Egoscue. He was a war veteran, awarded with a Purple Heart. He suffered chronic nerve pain and mobility issues due to battle wounds. Pete met with many medical experts, but none of them were able to fix the problems. Pain was his Life Challenge.

Pete began searching for a way to live pain-free. He didn't want to alleviate his symptoms, he wanted to fix the true cause —his posture and balance. Out of this challenge, was born his passion — the Egoscue Method of postural therapy.

As you complete the exercises in this chapter, don't write down what society or other people think you should do. Be your own detective and look objectively at what you're actually doing — not what you think you should be doing.

Please use the free downloadable workbook as you answer the following questions, while referring to the explanations in this chapter.

Workbook Question 2. What Passions have been drawn from your Life Challenges?

*****

WHAT LIGHTS YOU UP?

Close your eyes if you feel safe to do so, and think back to a moment when you felt really inspired and lit up in your home or work life. Relive that moment in your mind and feel the emotions bubbling up in your body.

Workbook Question 3. Describe specific moment(s) when you felt really inspired and lit up in your home and work life.

*****

HOW YOU FILL YOUR HOME AND WORKSPACE

Next, I'd like you to imagine a Detective coming into your home while you are out. They have never met you before and know nothing about you.

They go from room to room, noticing anything they feel must be of significant interest to you. They investigate the files on your home computer, check your phone, and everywhere else you store or consume digitally. Even the background on your phone and computer can give clues.

What will the Detective notice as key themes in your home?

Perhaps there are souvenir items from all the places you've travelled to. Travel guides on your bookshelf. A world map. A photo shrine containing your favourite holiday moments. Travel documentaries marked as watched on your TV player. The Detective would deduce that travelling all over the world is one of your Passions.

Alternatively, maybe your wall shrine is dedicated to photos of your children. There are children's things and trophies in every room. You also have many children's books, or parenting books. The Detective would deduce that children are one of your key Passions.

Conversely, while our children are very important to us, you will not find a significant number of items related to them outside of their bedrooms. So, although they are a priority, some Passions are more significant in our physical space.

The Detective would notice that we have a dedicated home gym. I have countless books on exercise and health on the bookshelf, and on kindle. There are vitamin supplements in the cupboard; more than the typical amount of athletic gear in the wardrobe; he'd find an assortment of yoga kit, blood pressure monitor and bodyfat scales. The Detective would correctly deduce that one of my Passions is "Health and Fitness."

What other Passions would he notice from the books I read, the podcasts and videos I watch, and the courses I've taken?

He'd see that Sarah and I have a very strong interest in property, investing, wealth, money and business. He'd also take note of a strong interest in personal development and spirituality.

Whilst children's items were not dominating the space, he'd notice a lot of books on parenting, family, building inspiring relationships with our children and on a romantic partner level. So, he might deduce "Family Relationships" to be a key Passion.

Also think about your workspace, or work locker. What would the Detective discover? What do you put on display? Maybe your screensaver indicates a passion?

Workbook Question 4. How do you fill your home and workspace?

*****

LEISURE ACTIVITIES YOU ENJOY THE MOST

Both Sarah and I really enjoy the process of learning, so we can grow and improve our lives. We are perpetual students. Therefore, we usually spend some time reading or doing courses every day. We don't need to work anymore, so if we're not going out for a day of fun, we will often spend most of the day learning and taking action on that learning. We sign up for multiple courses every year. If it's sunny, we spend our learning time sunbathing in the garden.

I also enjoy exercising regularly. Specifically, calisthenics, weights and yoga. Exercise always puts me into a meditative zone. I can't think about much else while I work out. Sarah tells me I get grumpy if I don't exercise due to illness or injury.

Sarah really enjoys preparing and cooking healthy food. Although I originally taught her to cook when we first met, she now does all the cooking and really loves it. Her Passion for cooking stems from two places. Firstly, she is providing for her family. Secondly, it hits our joint Passion for outstanding health.

We both spend a lot of time on spirituality. We meditate for 20-45 minutes every day and read about it. We both do a variety of the different types of yoga.

Think about the activities and tasks you enjoy the most in your leisure time. Consider how much time you actually spend on them, and how much they excite you. Perhaps when you are doing them you completely lose track of time?

Workbook Question 5. What activities or tasks do you do in your leisure time that you enjoy the most?

*****

WORK ACTIVITIES YOU ENJOY THE MOST

Some of the things I love to do are to help people to become financially free, happy, design their dream life, and contribute to others and the world.

I love teaching and coaching people. It's something I automatically do with my children — they often resist, but I can't help myself. I've also taught or coached people many times in previous jobs. I really like the direct interaction. It's such a great feeling watching people grow from an acorn to an oak tree, and celebrating their journey along the way.

Another part of previous jobs that I've always enjoyed doing, is the process of writing reports and presentations. That led to me writing books. I only write a book when I'm really passionate about a topic. I won't write a book for the sake of writing a book. I was so inspired to write this book, that it never felt like work and I frequently lost track of time. In fact, Sarah had to stop me from writing, so we could spend time doing other things.

Workbook Question 6. What activities do you do in your current job, or previous job, that you enjoy the most?

*****

HOW YOU SPEND YOUR MONEY

Now it's time to talk about money. Pull out your bank and credit card statements and take a peek. Write down any key themes you notice. If you're like Sarah and I, then you'll also need to look at your amazon order history!

By now, you are going to start to notice some patterns emerging in your workbook answers. That is a good thing. It means you've already begun incorporating your Passions into your lifestyle.

Workbook Question 7. How do you spend your money?

*****

WHAT YOU TALK ABOUT WITH FRIENDS

Sarah and I have a couple of main topics we always talk about. Namely property, investing, financial freedom, happiness, lifestyle design and purpose. We are always trying to make people's lives better. We can't help ourselves. We also talk a lot about health and fitness.

Finally, as we and most of our friends have children, we often swap parenting stories, etc.

Workbook Question 8. What do you love to talk about with friends?

*****

PASSION PRIORITY

Everyone prioritises their passions differently. The order should not be what society, or your spouse thinks is correct. It should be where you are actually focusing your attention in your life, right now.

Let me give you an example of how you we would answer. The number one most important thing is my relationship with Sarah. If that fails, then our family, our business, our money, and our entire life will go down the toilet! She is the glue that holds everything together. **But she is not number one in my Passions list!**

Why? Because that part feels stable to me. Hence my attention is mostly focused on other areas.

So, don't write your children at the top of the list, unless you are totally crazy about all things children and have picture shrines, talk endlessly about your kids, love playing with other people's kids, read books about kids and have completely built your life around your children. In fact, you worry what you will do when they leave home, as you have very few other interests.

Also, don't compare yourself to other people, and what they think you should do. You've had a unique set of experiences in your life. They are not you. If your children don't even feature on your Passions list, that is okay too. It doesn't mean you don't love them or make you a bad parent.

It's important to note that your Passions will change over time, depending on what's happening in your life. It may simply affect the ranking of your Passions, or you might introduce new ones.

Dr. John Demartini says, *"As you fill a void, a new void appears, generating a new value. Fulfilment of one value initiates a new dissatisfaction and a new void, which in turn drives you to new areas of fulfilment."*

Okay, time to reveal our current Passions list. Subject to change over time, of course.

George:
1 Financial Freedom
2 Spirituality
3 Family & Relationships
4 Health & Fitness

Sarah:
1 Family
2 Spirituality
3 Financial Freedom
4 Health & Vitality

I'm sure you'd guessed many of our Passions, following our examples for each question.

Firstly, notice that Sarah and I have a lot of overlap. If you are in are in a relationship, then it is helpful to have one or more identical Passions, so you can share those experiences together. But it's not necessary to have all four of them, virtually the same like us.

Sarah and I have them in a different order. She has 'Family' first. That's because she has the primary role of caregiver to our children. They've always turned to her first in times of stress. She takes care of everything related to their schooling, including school clothes, school trips, daily packed lunches, parent meetings, etc.

'Financial Freedom' has been higher for me previously due to the financial insecurity of my childhood, and my feelings of "not being good enough."

Sarah and I include each other and our children in the 'Family & Relationships' Passion.

'Spirituality' is not something we generally talk about with our friends, but it is something we focus on every day. I initially began meditating to reduce stress and come up with creative ideas. Things just gradually evolved from there. We are both on the path of 'enlightenment' together.

'Health and Fitness.' We both have a strong interest in health after suffering poor health and getting overweight in the past. My father passed away from Parkinson's, so optimum health is always on my mind.

The 'Fitness' element is mostly mine. I have a joy of exercising. Sarah mostly does it because she knows it's good for her.

My passion for exercising initially came from being bullied at school. I wanted to become strong and more muscular. By the time I was 15 years old, the bullying stopped. I had bigger muscles than most children and had low body fat.

However, my weight and health gradually went downhill, once I started working long hours in corporate life. At one point, my heart kept pausing multiple times a day.

It's your turn now.

Review your responses to questions 2-8 in your workbook and write down your top four Passions, in order of significance, with number one being the most significant.

If you only have one Passion, then that is okay too. Sarah and I are multi-Passioned. But you don't have to be — it is perfectly okay if you have less. You might have a strong, overwhelming, single Passion focus.

Workbook Question 9. What are your top 4 passions, in order of priority?

CHAPTER 4

Your Gifts

"Gifts" are the second variable in the Purpose Formula. You can apply your unique Gifts to your Passions.

Some of your Gifts may be very obvious to you. These are the things you do effortlessly, without thinking. They are the things your close friends and family know you're good at.

For example, I'm good with computers. I have a degree in Computer Science. When anything goes wrong on one of our computers in our home office, I fix it. When one of the kids is having a problem, I'm their "Tech Support."

Sometimes, just the effect of me walking into the room fixes their technology. Perhaps there are things unexplainable about your gifts too?

People have paid me in the past to set up their computer systems, and design websites. Although I don't do that anymore, it's something I'm naturally better at than most people. I learn new software easily. I'm not a tech specialist in any one thing, I'm just much better than most people at a lot of different things.

Note that computers and software are not my Passion. They are just tools I use.

Another of my gifts is writing. I've written a lot of reports and presentations throughout University and my working career.

However, it's also possible you don't know some of your gifts. So, it's really an eye opener, if you ask someone close to you.

When I asked Sarah, she told me my main gift was being a 'tweaker.' We eventually settled on 'optimiser' as a better word to describe my Gift. Once I thought about it, it was so blindingly obvious — I've been doing it my entire life! But I had no idea.

I love to fix my own and other people's lives. I use my Gift across all of my Passions. What I tend to do is research a topic really deeply — often thousands of hours of research. I experiment with trial and error, then then design the simplest, fastest, minimum effective dose required to achieve the goal. I love details, so I always include a lot of details in my work. As time goes on, I continually test and refine the system further, for even better results.

When you step back, you'll notice that I've applied this gift to all my books and my in-depth training courses. They contain decades of knowledge, condensed into an easy format.

If you were a fly on the wall in my home, you'll see that I've been optimising my diet, health and fitness for many years.

Sarah's Gifts are design, creativity and big picture thinking. She's an idea generator. She'll often meditate or go out for a walk and come back with loads of ideas. She's really great at 'out of the box' thinking and challenging norms. Sarah uses her gifts to help me to plan out the top-level structure of books and courses. Then I go to work on filling in the detail and writing them. It's a powerful combination.

Sarah also has the Gift of 'optimism.' She generally starts things with the faith that she will succeed, and that everything will work out in the end.

However, I have a brain that focuses on the practicality of implementation, projecting into the future and identifying failure points. With Sarah's optimism and my practicality, we have a nice balance. She throws up ideas and I rapidly test them out in my head.

Workbook Question 10. List your top three Gifts

Ask someone close to you if you can't list at least two of your Gifts.

FIND YOUR PURPOSE

Environment

CHAPTER 5

This is the next variable in the Purpose Formula. A significant change in your environment, can lead to a sudden and immediate change in your purpose. It could literally happen overnight.

Internal Environment

On an 'internal' level you need to look at your **physical body and mind.**

An example of a changing internal Environment could be cancer. If you were diagnosed with terminal cancer, and had only 12 months to live, then that would be a major factor on what you do with the rest of your year. It doesn't matter how passionate you are at being a teacher, doctor, or saving the environment.

But sometimes physical issues are there to be overcome, in a truly inspiring way.

FIND YOUR PURPOSE

Nineteen-year-old Dani Burt woke up from a motorbike accident, to find her right leg had been amputated. Not only that, but she had a ruptured spleen, her left arm was paralysed, and she had severe internal bleeding. Her brain was injured, so she had to have speech and language therapy.

After a lot of rehabilitation, she eventually decided to try surfing for fun. She'd never done it before, but she quickly became really good at it. One day, someone came up to her and asked her to compete in a competition in Hawaii. She won third place. That got her hooked. In 2017 Dani was crowned the women's World Adaptive Surfing Champion.

Dani's purpose is to *"advocate for equality in surfing"*. In 2018, she was able to encourage The International Surfing Association to rectify its rules and regulations to exclude gender discrimination.

*****

Being overweight and unhealthy is another example of your Internal Environment. Sarah remembers the time she had just bought a new pair of PJs' in size 16-18…and they didn't fit! She said, *"I was too fat. I was disgusted with myself, and how far I'd let myself go. I looked at a recent photo of me and felt even more disgust. I was at my lowest point. I said to myself, 'no more!'"*

Sarah knew she'd been massively overeating since having two young children so close in age. It was very

ENVIRONMENT

stressful, and almost like having twins. She felt a lot of shame about overeating and eating in secret. But she had hit rock bottom and needed my help…so one day she told me everything.

I was really shocked when she confessed that she secretly ate jars chocolate spread and biscuits, whenever our children were napping. She knew it wasn't healthy, but she used it to numb and reward herself. I had no idea what had been going on while I was working. She also felt that if she continued down her current path, that she would suffer from major health problems, which would impact our children.

Feeling depressed, repulsed, but motivated to transform, she made her new purpose to *"Get control of my eating and lose weight for me and my family."*

I put together a weight training programme for Sarah and we devised some general meal plans. I personally trained her four times a week, in the evening, when our kids were asleep. We threw out all the ingredients to make biscuits and cakes, and other junk food. We planned to eat only whole food from now on. I became her accountability buddy.

Over the next 18 months, Sarah lost an amazing four stone (56 pounds), and she looked in the best shape of her life. As a side effect of changing our healthier eating habits, I lost 21 lbs. We both realised how easy it was to let your bodyfat creep up each month, so we made health and fitness a core part of our passions.

Other internal environmental issues could be overcoming addictions, or improving mental health issues such as depression or anxiety. Focusing on them for a period of time can really make an enormous difference to you and your family's lives.

Workbook Question 11. Are there any factors in your Internal environment (Mind/Body), which could affect your purpose?

Maslow's Hierarchy of Needs

Maslow created the model to describe how the motivational behaviours of people generally changed as their needs were met. He created five levels.

SELF ACTUALISATION — Desire to reach your full potential. Spirituality.

ESTEEM — Dignity, achievement, mastery, independence, recognition, status.

LOVE & BELONGING — Human connection, friendship and being part of a group or community.

SAFETY — Health, personal security, emotional security and financial security.

PHYSIOLOGICAL — Survival elements: air, water, heat, food, shelter, sexual needs.

Physiological needs — if you don't have the basic survival elements like air, water, heat, food, shelter and sleep, then it is difficult to think about anything else. Your day-to-day survival is at stake. Maslow also included sexual needs at that level, as it is such a basic biological urge.

Safety Needs — this includes your health, personal security, emotional security and financial security. For example, if you're in a war zone, or experiencing domestic violence, then your personal security is of primary concern to you. If you don't have a job or are on a very low income and can't afford to buy enough food, then that could also be a factor.

Love and Belonging needs — Belonging can be thought of as human connection, friendship and being part of a group or community.

Esteem needs — these could be split into two areas: those you obtain from yourself, and those from others.

The esteem you feel for yourself, includes dignity, achievement, mastery and independence.

Secondly, the respect you feel from others — which can include recognition and status. Maslow stated that the need to feel respected, must be achieved in children before they can meet their self-esteem needs.

I'd like to add my personal experience with regard to 'status.' You can't buy it!

For many years, I attempted to feel worthy and improve my self-esteem, by purchasing and wearing luxury designer clothes — even though I could not afford them. These things did nothing for my esteem. I still felt unworthy. It was only when I finally became wealthy and discovered that I did not need to wear flashy clothes to prove anything, that I finally realised that 'esteem' comes from inside you.

Self-Actualisation Needs — this sits at the top of the pile. It's the desire to reach your full potential as a human being.

Our experience with Maslow's model: My wife and I are mostly focused on the Self-actualisation stage. We have everything we need. We have enough money, a nice house, human connection and autonomy. We invest a lot of time on personal development and spirituality. We enjoy growing our knowledge in all areas of our life. We also help other people to improve their lives.

However, like most people, we have low mood days. Perhaps we receive an unexpected large bill, have a health scare, or one of our children is struggling with school or their friends, and our "need level" drops to Safety. Whatever happens, these temporary setbacks are on our mind day and night, until we rise above them, and get back to Self-actualisation.

We've always been into personal development, to improve all areas of our lives — financial, health, fitness, family and spiritual. So even if you are mostly focusing on the Safety needs at the moment, there's nothing to stop you from including some time on personal development in your daily routine. Our continual thirst for knowledge, plus inspired action is the reason we'd achieved so much at a young age. You're reading this book right now, which is already time spent in the Self-Actualisation level — so well done YOU!

It's never too early to start expanding your knowledge. Elon Musk, Billionaire and CEO of Tesla and Space X, said he read the entire Encyclopaedia Britannica at age nine.

Workbook Question 12. What level are you at in Maslow's Hierarchy of Needs and what would you need to improve to get to the next level?

EXTERNAL ENVIRONMENT

Home life — Changes in your home life can affect your purpose. Tiger Woods watched his father playing golf when he was 6 months old and started playing when he was 2 years old. That led to him becoming one of the best golfers of all time.

Work life — Changes in your work can affect your purpose too. Perhaps a new opportunity appears…or your job becomes dissatisfying. It may be that what was once a really passionate career, now has no room for growth and seems dull. Or perhaps the working environment, culture, or people aren't enjoyable anymore.

Macro factors, known by the acronym PESTLE, can also affect your purpose:

Political – changes in government and other associations. War.

Economic — changes in the market structure, tax, interest rates and other economic indicators.

Sociocultural — changes in demographics, culture, attitudes, or current issues.

Technological — technological innovations and increased adoption.

Legal — new laws and regulatory bodies

Environmental — negative effects of climate change, adverse weather, conservation, natural resources.

ENVIRONMENT

You may be thinking, how can these factors outside of my control, affect my Purpose?

Let's look at an example of how Environmental changes can affect you. 15-year-old Greta Thunberg protested outside the Swedish parliament in 2018, holding a sign saying, "School Strike for Climate." Her campaign spread across the world. Now Greta has millions of followers on social media. Her purpose seems to be, to challenge world leaders to take action for climate change.

And now for a political environmental change. In Man's Search for Meaning, Viktor Frankl chronicled his experiences as a prisoner in Nazi concentration camps, during World War II. Death was a daily occurrence. He recounted the numerous times he stood next to dead bodies, and felt no emotion. Every day might be his last.

"The emaciated bodies of the sick were thrown on two-wheeled carts which were drawn by prisoners for many miles, often through snowstorms, to the next camp. If one of the sick men had died before the cart left, he was thrown on anyway—the list had to be correct. The list was the only thing that mattered. A man counted only because he had a prison number. One literally became a number: dead or alive—that was unimportant;"

Even in these horrific conditions, Viktor and the other prisoners discovered their purpose:

"Every man was controlled by one thought only: to keep himself alive for the family waiting for him at home, and to save his friends."

Change Your Environment

Sometimes you are living your true purpose, however it is just your working environment that is the problem. For example, let's say you're a nurse in a hospital and absolutely love talking with and helping your patients every day. You've wanted to be a nurse since you were a child. The job used to bring you so much joy, but now you dread going to work.

Perhaps working conditions have deteriorated, or there are colleagues making your work miserable? If you believe that helping people by being a nurse is your purpose, then changing department, hospital or to a different type of clinic could bring you back to fulfilment and happiness.

Seasons of Purpose Model

We created this four-stage model to explain how your focus changes through your lifetime. The ages are only a guide, as to what might be going on in your life at that stage. What's far more important, are the activities you're doing.

SEASONS OF PURPOSE MODEL

SPRING Discovery 0-25 years	SUMMER Growth 25-50 years	AUTUMN Harvest 50-75 years	WINTER Wisdom 75-100 years
Experiment with passions, education and careers	Expand education, career, business, relationships, family, wealth	Consolidate, simplify and reap your harvest of money, business and relationships	Lead business and family. Work only on passion projects. Share wisdom

SPRING: Discovery
You focus on your education and getting your first jobs. It is a time of discovery and experimentation. Finding out what careers you like, and what personally interests you. It's a time for taking risks — using your supportive parents as a safety net.

SUMMER: Growth
You expand your education, career, or business. You increase your wealth, relationships and may start a family.

AUTUMN: Harvest
Now is the time to "milk your cash cows," or reap your harvest. You stop expanding and reap your rewards.

Consolidate and simplify your business, money and relationships — remove what is not working for you. You'll have more freedom and your children will move out of the family home.

WINTER: Wisdom
Working less or retiring. Focusing on your passion projects. Imparting your wisdom (e.g. taking over from your parents as the leader of your multi-generational family, or sitting on the board of a company, instead of being the CEO).

Eliminate or reduce risks, to maintain what you have achieved in your life. You prepare your legacy and begin succession planning training for your children and business. Contribute your wisdom to others by mentoring them.

MOVING BETWEEN SEASONS
You don't necessarily need to head towards Winter — although that's what most people do. It's also possible to shift back one or more seasons. For example, when we became financially free, Sarah was only 39 years old.

We stopped growing for two years, while we sat in 'Autumn.' This led us to feeling unfulfilled. So after that, we moved back to focusing mostly on Summer, and bought more investment properties.

Workbook Question 13. Which level are you at in the Seasons of Purpose model, and are there any elements you want to do more of?

ARE YOU PUTTING MONEY AHEAD OF YOUR HEALTH?

> *"If you have no health,*
> *then you have no business."*
> *— George Choy*

You'll notice in the chapter on Passions that one of our top four is Health. It's been a priority for Sarah and me for many years.

People tend to start experiencing medical problems from age 40 onwards (Summer). By age 65 (Autumn) most people have at least one long-term medical condition. Why wait? Start to find ways to get interested in improving your health now.

I speak to many people who've not had health in their list for a good proportion of their lives. Sadly, it jumps to the top of their list when they start to have health issues and are diagnosed with various ailments. It's far easier and cheaper to prevent problems now, than to fix them in your fifties.

FIND YOUR PURPOSE

CHAPTER 6

Ultimate Life Vision (ULV)

"The future belongs to those who believe in the beauty of their dreams."
— Eleanor Roosevelt

Having an exciting vision of your future is so important. If you have nothing to look forward to, then you have no reason to live.

I experienced extreme depression towards the end of my corporate career. I worked long hours and often travelled at the weekend, for a meeting on Monday morning. I barely saw my children, who were toddlers at the time…or Sarah.

I travelled a lot internationally. It seemed glamorous to begin with, but it very quickly turned into travelling to the airport on my own; sitting in the airport on my own; eating dinner on my own; sleeping in a hotel on my own; having a meeting, and then another lonely trip back home late at night. I felt so lonely and tired.

When the stress of work and office politics became unbearable, I fell into massive depression. I withdrew from life.

I couldn't leave my job. My family relied on the income to pay the bills. I continued going to work like a drone. I couldn't see any way out. I didn't have anything to look forward to. There was no compelling future for me.

Sarah could see I was really unhappy. Our relationship was tense. One day, we were sitting in a café, while our children were playing in the soft play. Sarah encouraged me to open up to her. I was resistant at first, but eventually told her how miserable I was. She was shocked at how I'd kept it to myself, and how serious things had become.

She gave me permission to quit my job — right there and then. We had no idea how we would pay the bills. But as the endless optimist, she believed we would find a way.

I handed in my notice of resignation the next day. While I didn't have a clear idea of my future at that point, the clouds lifted, and I started to appreciate life again.

*****

Your Ultimate Life Vision

Designing your ULV is something that Sarah and I do and it's so awesome. It gives you clear direction for your life, which you can start heading towards now.

Ask yourself, what would your ULV look like? What kind of things would you like to be doing in a typical week? It's useful to build this picture in your mind.

When building your ULV, you should think it through — like trying on a hat.

For example, I briefly flirted with the idea of becoming an International speaker. Once I started to really think through the lifestyle, such as travelling to up to five different events in a week and living out of a suitcase, I quickly realised that the life of a full-time professional speaker was not for me. I've done the corporate travelling gig, and it made me feel extremely lonely and depressed. However, other people will be really excited and thrive on that lifestyle — particularly if they enjoy meeting and speaking with lots of new people every week.

What should you include in your ULV? It's whatever you want. There is no right or wrong. Your best life is far out in the future. Perhaps ten or twenty years away. People underestimate how much they can achieve over that time. So don't hold back, and don't worry about the large gap between where you are now, and where you want to get to.

Perhaps consider some practical things, like:

- How much you earn, where you'll be living, the type of house you'll be living in, and the car you'll drive.

- What else will you own?

- If you don't have children at the moment, and it's one of your dreams, then how many will you have?

- Will you get married?

- What will you have achieved?

- If you're unhappy with your body at the moment, then what does it look and feel like?

- What issues in your current life would be fixed?

- What will you be doing every day?

I'd strongly recommend you include some element of contribution, to create a fulfilling life.

Workbook Question 14. Describe your Ultimate Life Vision.

*****

YOUR ULTIMATE SELF

You didn't get to your ULV by accident. You had to become a certain sort of person to get there.

You might need have to have certain behaviours, habits, beliefs and achievements. Here are a couple of questions to get the juices flowing…

- What kinds of things would your Ultimate Self need to do regularly?

ULTIMATE LIFE VISION (ULV)

- What will it take to become that person?

- What skills would they have mastered?

- What would they believe?

- What would they have in their life?

- How would they earn, invest and spend their money?

Workbook Question 15. Ultimate Self — What kind of person do you need to be, to achieve your Ultimate Life Vision?

APPRECIATING THE JOURNEY

Most people are all so eager to get to the next level, that they rarely appreciate what they have already. If you ever feel that you have nothing in your life to be grateful for, then think of Viktor Frankl. He was held prisoner in Nazi concentration camps, where every day could be his last. He recounts:

> *"Standing outside we saw sinister clouds glowing in the west and the whole sky alive with clouds of ever-changing shapes and colors, from steel blue to blood red. The desolate grey mud huts provided a sharp contrast, while the puddles on the muddy ground reflected the glowing sky. Then, after minutes of moving silence, one prisoner said to another, "How beautiful the world could be.""*
> — *Viktor Frankl, Man's Search For Meaning*

FIND YOUR PURPOSE

I'd like to share a story with you.

Imagine you're taking a trip to Sydney, Australia.

You pack your suitcases, flight tickets, and then drive to London Heathrow airport. You're filled with excitement about going on this journey.

With a bound in your step and a radiant smile, you arrive at the airport and go to the check in desk. You get a delightful surprise when you are upgraded to business class. You do a little shopping and then head over to the business lounge to relax, eat a few snacks and drink a glass of prosecco, while you wait for your flight.

On the plane, you look out the window with awe as you fly above all the houses, forests and green lands. The ground disappears and you fly above the clouds. The world is a wonderous place.

You settle down to a couple of movies and have a glass of red wine with your dinner. Then you put on your eye mask and recline the flat bed seat — dreaming of Sydney.

The plane lands and you are excited to transfer at Singapore Changi Airport — one of the best airports in the world. You go to a spa for a back and neck massage, then visit some of the wonderous gardens and other attractions in the airport. You're enjoying yourself so much, that you barely noticed the call to board the plane for Sydney.

ULTIMATE LIFE VISION (ULV)

On the plane, you rest on another business class seat and shortly you have a noodle meal and settle down to another couple of movies.

Finally, you arrive at Sydney and are filled with excitement and anticipation as you step off the airplane.

The trip to Sydney is much like your Ultimate Life Vision. It is the destination you are really excited to get to. There will be many steps along the way, and much to enjoy as you get closer, and closer.

If you take action to make your ULV happen, you may get there much sooner than you think. But always look around and be grateful for your current situation, knowing that you are on your way.

Happiness is in the now.

CHAPTER 7

12-Month Goals

"Setting goals is the first step in turning the invisible into the visible."
— Tony Robbins

Sarah and I have achieved so much more than we ever dreamed possible:

- Financially free when Sarah was only 39, never needing to work again.

- Own a multi-million residential and commercial property empire.

- Have travelled all over the world.

- Have 2 amazing kids that provide us with joy and challenge every day.

- We've written books.

What made us so successful?

Apart from spending our life continually learning and developing, the other secret weapon we have is setting goals.

When we take a look through past goals, we achieved nearly everything we wrote down. One of the reasons for that is the good old Reticular Activating System (RAS) — it literally puts opportunities to achieve your goals, right in front of you.

Powerful eh? You can literally manifest your life.

We set goals once a year and tick them off as we achieve them. We keep a record of goals achieved, rather than deleting them, so we can celebrate our achievements at the end of the year. Sarah and I have a combined set of goals.

Our goal list evolves throughout the year. We often add new goals when we achieve one of them. Or we might delete a goal if we had a change of strategy and it is no longer of interest to us.

I study our goals every Monday morning, to make sure I'm on track.

As you think about setting your own 12-month goals, I recommend from experience, that you don't set goals that are so far beyond where you are now, that your mind immediately can't believe it and shouts BS!

For instance, if you currently have mountains of credit card debt, and you put your goal to be a billionaire within a year, then you'll feel defeated before you even

12-MONTH GOALS

start the journey. Your brain thinks it is an impossible goal.

For example, let's say you're in your ULV, you wrote that you own over £1 million worth of investment properties, and are financially free. But, perhaps you don't own any investment properties at the moment. So, one of your 12-month goals could be to buy ONE investment property.

If you are currently overweight, but in your Best Life you weigh 140 lbs, then you might set yourself a target amount of weight to lose in the first year. Perhaps 2 lbs a month, to be ultra-conservative. You might set yourself a minimum number of steps each day, or which days of the week you will exercise, etc. You can also have a goal to put together an exercise programme and meal plan.

Or maybe in your ULV you're a Nomadic Travel Vlogger, who has visited 193 countries. Your 12-month goals might include starting the vlog and travelling to one country every few months, and setting up jobs to fund it along the way, like farm work, etc.

If you've always dreamed of having children, but have been putting it off for years, then trying to get pregnant in the next 12-months might be your goal.

I recommend you choose a maximum of ten goals. They should be the ones that will move the needle, and take you a few steps closer to achieving your ULV. As your ULV includes all areas of your life, not just money or business, your ten goals should cover these areas as well.

Another important point is that goals should be something you can either control (i.e. a new habit you instigate), or strongly influence. Goals such as winning the lottery are not particularly constructive.

Once you achieve each goal, you can set a new one in that area, to move closer to your vision.

Workbook Question 16. Take a look at your responses to the Ultimate Life Vision questions and put together some goals to achieve within 12 months from now, that will take you a step closer to your ULV.

CHAPTER 8

Identity

"Knowing yourself is the beginning of all wisdom."
— Aristotle

We all have multiple identities. Father, mother, husband, wife, son, daughter, job, gym hero, yogi, writer, vlogger, the list goes on and on…

However, only one of those identities dominates your persona. On a simplistic level, your key 'Identity' could be how you introduce yourself to others, or how you think of yourself in your mind.

Your key identity can either guide you to an inspiring life…or crush it.

I might say, "Hi, I'm George. I'm a Property Investor, and Author."

Or you might introduce yourself as a "Mum."

When I asked my eleven-year-old son, he said "I'm a gamer."

But it goes deeper than that. We need to search for the real meaning in your Identity.

Another way of thinking about it, is imagining your life is a movie. What's the identity of your character?

When I worked in the corporate world, one of my identities was my marketing job title. But it was more than that…I was a "Corporate Career Man."

All I wanted to do, was keep increasing my skills and experience, so I could get promoted up the ranks. My primary aim was to make more money, and feel significant from the status. I was the breadwinner in our family, so they all relied on me.

Workbook Question 17. What is your current (or last) Identity?

3-Step Identity Transition Protocol

On the day I handed in my resignation notice and quit my corporate career, with no job to go to, I felt completely lost. I didn't know who I was now. The money was gone. My status was gone. I was a nobody.

I was in Phase 2 (Decision) of the *Five Phases of Purpose* model, from chapter one. I barely slept for a few weeks…my mind kept asking, "who am I now?"

All I knew was that I didn't want to go back to my old job. But I now had a hole in my personality. It felt like part of me was missing and needed to be filled.

I experienced the same thing when Sarah and I became financially free. I was not the breadwinner anymore. Our properties were owned equally, so we both received the income and did very little work for it. I almost felt like I was not needed anymore. I served no purpose.

At the time, I had no way of coping with losing my identity.

Since then, I've developed a 3-Stage Identity Transition Protocol, to help process this loss.

IDENTITY TRANSITION PROTOCOL

(3) GRATITUDE
List all the ways your previous identity benefitted you

(2) SHAKE IT OFF
Dance and shake off the negative feelings

(1) JOURNAL IT OUT
Pour out your negative feelings and emotions until there is nothing left to say

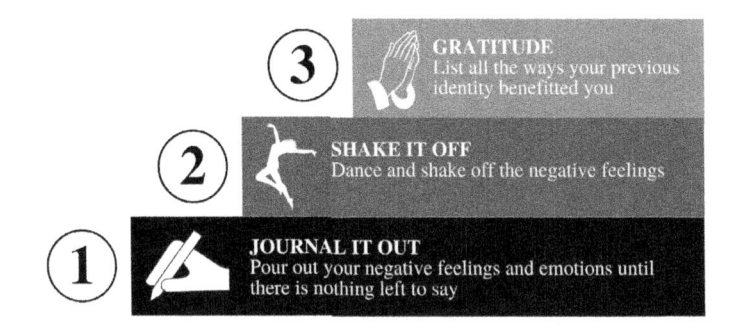

Step 1: Journal it out
Get a sheet of paper and write down everything you are FEELING inside. You are going to destroy it afterwards. Pour out your negative feelings and emotions until there is nothing left to say. This is really important for processing it. If you prefer to write it on your computer and delete it afterwards, that is ok too.

Write down everything that that upsets you about this loss of identity. It might be how specific people behaved negatively towards you, or events that happened, or even grief. Write down whatever negative feelings you have…and keep writing until you've got it out of you. It's okay to keep repeating the same words or phrases. Just let all your thoughts turn into writing.

If you prefer to visualise it instead of writing, or say it in your head, or out loud, then do that. Whatever feels right, for you.

Doing this will temporarily make you feel worse, but that's okay, as you are trying to get it all out of your head. Whatever you think of, is fine to write down. It's for your eyes only.

That was tough. Give yourself some love and hug yourself. You're going to be okay. Everything will work out the way it is meant to be.

Step 2: Shake it off
It's time for some dance therapy. This will act as a pattern interrupt from the negative thinking, and boost your mood. Hence, it should be carried out immediately after your journaling.

Animals regularly shake themselves. When something happens to them, like accidentally falling over, or when they wake up, they often get up and shake it off.

So, find a clear area with plenty of space. Close the curtains, put on some music and dance around. Imagine you are covered in a disgusting goo or mud and are trying to shake it off you. Shake your hands, arms, legs. Shake it off, until you feel you have got the bad energy out of you. I really enjoy doing this to 'Shake It Off', by Taylor Swift. But, play whatever music feels right for you and how you are feeling. If you want to punch the air or cushions, go for it! If you get the urge to scream into a cushion, do that too.

If you have some kind of injury or physical condition that prevents you from doing this, or causes pain, then adapt the exercise so that it is safe for you, and will not cause further injury.

Step 3: Gratitude
This can seem like the most difficult part. No matter how bad or numb your feelings may be towards your previous identity, there will always be some good.

Look beyond the bad things and only focus on the positive. There will always be some benefits, if you look objectively enough.

For example, did it help you to learn a specific skill?

Perhaps you earned the highest amount of money so far in your life?

Or you met someone at work who is now your best friend, or spouse?

Or you learned what you do NOT want to be doing, going forward.

Workbook Question 18. List of all the ways your last identity benefitted you. How is this shifting identity helping you? What can you be grateful for?

Come up with as many benefits as you can. Twenty to fifty would be ideal.

*****

Workbook Question 19. List all the things you really enjoyed doing as part of your last Identity.

*****

YOUR NEW IDENTITY

Have a think about what you would like your new identity to be. This is an identity you will adopt for use now.

Sometimes it's just a little enhancement to the wording of your current identity. Imagine trying on the Identity, like a new hat. How does it feel?

But, if you really have no idea at all, then don't worry. That's okay. You can come back to it when you've nailed down your purpose.

Workbook Question 20. What is your new Identity?

CHAPTER 9

Your Driving Question

You may not have consciously realised it, but there is a question you ask yourself multiple times a day.

This question shapes your life. It leads the decisions you make every day, and can leave you feeling inspired…or continually frustrated and disappointed.

How do you give birth to your Driving Question? Often, it's the result of a Life Challenge you've experienced. It may go all the way back to your childhood.

Most people's Driving Question is negative, or destructive. They have a question like …

- "Why do bad things always happen to me?"

- "Why am I always broke?"

- "Why does everything I do fail?"

- "Why am I so stupid?"

Guess what happens in your life due to your Driving Question. Your RAS will continually look for proof that it's true, and bring it to your attention. You'll see it evidence everywhere you look, all day long.

Also note that many of negative the examples I gave, contain the words "always," or" everything." If those phrases are used in a negative question, then it becomes an all-encompassing belief. Your mind believes that this will be correct, every single time. There will never be a case when the opposite happens. That sucks as a way to live.

In contrast, if you use those two words in a positive question, then it will have a positive effect.

Workbook Question 21. Write down your current Driving Question.

*****

HOW TO CREATE A NEW DRIVING QUESTION

Tony Robbins' original question was: *"How can I make it better?"*

At first glance, it seems quite innocent.

But if something prevented him from making something better, such as lack of time, resources, or something else, then it would make him crazy. So, Tony changed it to *"How can I experience even more of God's perfection in this moment?"* That helped him to look for the good in every situation.

My Driving Question also wasn't a healthy one. It used to be: *"How can I make more money?"* It was loaded with an emotional feeling of a lack of money.

It was born out of the time when I barely had enough money to pay the bills, and felt desperate. I was so stressed about being able to feed our children, and pay our mortgage, so our house didn't get repossessed. Money was on my mind, day and night.

It wasn't a healthy Driving Question to have. Even when I was relaxing, the question would pop into my mind. If money hadn't come in that day, I'd be continually thinking about what action I could take right now, to get some more money in the bank. I ended up doing a lot of busywork that delivered very little results.

I had the same Driving Question for many years, even after I became financially free. It left me feeling continually anxious and stressed about money.

Then one day I decided to change my Driving Question to something more positive — *"How can I experience joy or fulfilment right now?"*

My new question is so much better for my mental health. I feel relaxed and happy when it pops into my mind. It steers what I do with my time. I've stopped doing, or reduced some of the things I found less enjoyable. My days are now flowing with so much fulfilment and joy.

When a new opportunity presents itself, I now ask myself whether it will bring me joy or fulfilment, before agreeing to it.

The many hours I spent writing this book, provided me with great fulfilment. I never needed to be reminded to write every day. I was inspired to write it. I knew it was important to get this book out to the world, to help people like me, who went through this purpose crisis.

Sarah's Driving Question is: *"What do I need to do now?"*

This question formed in her mind when she was 11 years old. She had a spelling test at a school, where they frequently shamed poor performers. She was amongst the bottom four people on that particular test.

That created her belief, that if she doesn't get everything done, and do it better than everyone else…then she's not good enough. She's not worthy.

While Sarah's question came from a negative experience, she's still keeping hold of it, as it helps her to get so much done. She admits, it's not perfect, as it can make it difficult for her to relax. She also gets frustrated when she's relying on other people to take action, and she has to wait.

Improvements for Sarah's question could be to add something to the end of it, to make it broader, and to allow her to take care of herself. For example:

"What do I need to do now for my money, family, or happiness?"

Or *"What can I choose to do now?",* which can include relaxing, reading, self-care etc.

The good news is that you can reprogram your mind.

Once I'd come up with my new Driving Question, I just repeated it over and over again. I wrote it on a sticky note on my computer monitor. When I was walking, I just kept repeating it in my mind, like a mantra. I said it in the shower.

Every time my old question accidentally came up, I'd repeat my new question multiple times. Repetition changed it for me in a week. It may take less or more time for you, depending on how many times you repeat it.

The quality of your question determines the quality of your life. If you every feel angry or frustrated, ask yourself whether your feelings in this situation are due to your old Driving Question — then repeat your new question a few times.

If you feel that your current question is a positive influence on your life, then perhaps, like Sarah you might choose to keep it or tweak it to make it more helpful or healthy. Often the question can have served you in the past, or at least meant well.

But if you don't like what it is doing to you, and the negative emotion surrounding it, then create a new question to change your life.

I urge you to keep your new Driving Question short, and written in your personal words.

This is not some kind of public mission statement with formal words. It must have meaning to you. It needs to be really easy for you to remember, and say in your head.

Workbook Question 22. What is your new Driving Question?

CHAPTER 10

The 6 Human Needs and Contribution

Our daily decisions are not only driven by our Driving Question, but also our focus on the 6 Human Needs. We all have the same six needs. But how you focus on them, and in what order, can determine your life. It's why we do, what we do. It can explain your habits, relationships, interests, and every decision you make. I was introduced to this concept by Tony Robbins.

The 6 Human Needs are:

1. Certainty

2. Uncertainty/Variety

3. Significance

4. Love and Connection

5. Growth

6. Contribution

The last of those needs, "Contribution" is the most significant, as it is the final variable in the Purpose Formula.

Everyone is unique and will have more focus on some needs over the others. Those more powerful needs are your core needs.

Many of the activities you do, fulfil more than one need. Habits, particularly addictive and unhealthy habits, quite often fulfil three or more needs. For instance, smoking could light up your needs for certainty, significance and connection with other smokers.

As you read through the descriptions, have a think about how you meet each of these needs in your life, both positively and negatively. Also, which ones are by far the strongest drivers in your life right now.

1. Certainty

It's your need to feel safe and secure. To have a reliable outcome of pain or pleasure. You like planning, schedules and to do lists. You may be trustworthy and always do what you tell people you will do. You want your life to remain the same, which is impossible.

Perhaps you have a strong need for financial certainty. You need that regular salary, otherwise your life falls apart. The idea of running your own business, or doing contract work sounds scary to you.

Maybe you have the need to control your environment. You like everything to be in the same place. You eat the same meals. You feel uneasy about going on holiday.

You might have rituals, or addictive, or obsessive behaviours.

I have a strong need for financial security, in that I never want to go back to having a stressful job again. The idea of returning to the workplace is one of my recurring nightmares, which rears its head every now and then. So, staying financially free is really important to me.

Sarah has a very high need for Certainty. She feels like she needs to control everything in her life, so she doesn't fail. Otherwise she will "not be good enough." This is strongly linked to her Driving Question of: "What do I need to do now?" She is working on this!

Certainty can also fuel negative habits. Perhaps you self-medicate with food or alcohol whenever you feel low — it's a way you've taught yourself to temporarily numb the pain. Or perhaps you are a smoker – it is a tool you use to relax when you feel stressed.

Workbook Question 23. List the main ways you achieve Certainty in your life. Positive and negative.

2. Uncertainty/Variety

People who have this as one of their core needs, tend to get bored easily. They like to go to new places, meet new people, frequently change jobs. They can be spontaneous and impulsive. Relationships might not last, because you enjoy the thrill of new relationships.

You might not be good at planning, and often turn up late, as you lose track of time. People may feel you are unreliable.

You'll generally be outgoing and love meeting new people. You might have lots of interests and activities that you like to do.

On the negative side of variety, you might be an adrenaline junkie, or take excessive risks, because you just like the thrill of seeing what will happen. You might have trouble maintaining relationships because you continually start arguments or act unpredictably.

Children are also a good source of variety. Most days with our kids are great. But sometimes, particularly when getting ready for school in the morning, it's like shaking a magic 8 ball, to see what mood they're in. Whether it's a new teacher, new subject, examination, or friend issues — there always seems to be a new challenge to keep us on our toes.

I achieve variety through my exercise. I usually devise a workout routine and follow it for a couple of months, then get bored and change it.

Sarah and I both like to have three to four "projects" on the go at the same time, to stop us from getting bored. This could be anything, such as buying a property, redecorating our home, writing a book, creating a vlog, or planning a holiday.

Other ways we achieve variety are by regularly going for days out while our kids are at school. We often go for meals out, the cinema, sightseeing and spend the day at a spa. We love learning, so we read multiple books every week and participate in courses to improve different areas of our life.

Workbook Question 24. List the main ways you achieve Uncertainty/Variety in your life. Positive and negative.

3. Significance

This is the need to feel important to other people. It is not unusual for men to have a slightly higher need for significance than women. It's part of that natural instinct for men to compete against each other.

Significance can range from having your children dependent on you, being in a relationship, to being in charge of others at work, or wanting to present on stage in front of thousands of people. You want to feel special — to have recognition.

Sarah and I are highly driven to succeed. We enjoy achieving goals. I enjoy studying for certifications. We are also highly competitive. I'm a perfectionist, but I've managed to reel it in a little over the last few years. These are all signs of feeding our needs for significance.

I achieve significance through my children, Sarah, mentoring, my weekly vlogs and the books I write. Occasionally we get asked to pose in a photo with someone, which we can't deny, gives us both a little buzz.

There are also negative and unhealthy ways of gaining significance. These are all at the subconscious level. People don't realise why they are doing it.

In my 20s and 30s I dressed only in designer labels and had tailored suits, to increase my status. Upon reflection, this was due to my feelings of feeling inferior and poor growing up. 'Dressing the part' did not make me rich…it made me broke! It was only when I became financially free, that I realised I did not need to display my wealth anymore. Self-worth comes from within.

Children can throw tantrums to gain attention. Some people might enjoy starting arguments.

People who say negative comments about people's actions on social media are subconsciously trying to fill their need for significance — even if they feel fully justified due to their beliefs, situation or trauma. Deep down they want to prove that they are right, and therefore become more significant.

Individuals with medical conditions and pain may talk about it all the time, and justify that their pain or disability is worse than someone else's. They do not realise it, but they are trying to fill their need for significance too.

For those people with a really strong need for Significance, it can bring out the worst behaviour in people. There are also those that crave money, power or fame at all costs, and have either lied, or manipulated people to fill their need.

Take a moment to be critical of yourself. If you've ever displayed some of these negative needs for significance, have a think about how you could fulfil your need for significance in alternative, more positive ways.

Workbook Question 25. List the main ways you achieve Significance in your life. Positive and negative.

The next three Human Needs are the needs of the soul. They will provide you with the most joy and the most fulfilment in life. These three should be your main focus in life.

4. LOVE AND CONNECTION

You may constantly seek out a close relationship and devote yourself to them. Your relationships are really fulfilling. Perhaps you take part in group hobbies, team sports, or religious worship, to feel connected.

Your place of work can also give you connection to colleagues and customers.

Sarah and I get love through: each other and through our children, close family, and our cat. We gain "connection" through our friends, social media, yoga community and Sarah is in a choir.

On the negative side of Love and Connection — you might become so infatuated with someone, that you literally can't think of anything else and sacrifice all your needs for them.

Some people do not actively seek out love. If you've been hurt in love before, you might actively push people away. Connection may all you may be able to handle until you have addressed and processed your trauma.

If Love and Connection is a low need for you, then you might find people a distraction, and prefer computers and machines. You probably hate going to meetings and enjoy being on your own.

However, everyone has some need for love and connection, and will meet it somehow. Virtual online connection is better than nothing – thank goodness for Zoom for keeping us in touch with people in the absence of alternatives in the past few years.

Workbook Question 26. List the main ways you achieve Love and Connection in your life. Positive and negative.

5. GROWTH

If you're not growing, you're dying. Growth helps you to do more, and be more. It could include learning new things, achieving bigger goals, or stretching your boundaries. The most growth occurs at the boundary where you feel fairly uncomfortable.

Perhaps your work enables you to learn new skills, or take on more and more responsibility.

Sarah and I have such a strong need for growth. We spend time learning every single day, and are on a never-ending journey, to improve all aspects of our lives — property, business, money, relationships, family, health, fitness, yoga and spirituality. We set ourselves bigger goals every year, to stretch our boundaries.

Growth can also happen inside you. For example, growing spiritually, releasing trauma, and even reading this book and creating a more fulfilling life.

There can be negative aspects too. If you keep going back to university or higher education to study more and more, but don't apply anything in your life, then you're essentially drifting rather than truly growing.

Workbook Question 27. List the main ways you achieve Growth in your life. Positive and negative.

6. CONTRIBUTION

> *"The secret to living is giving."*
> *– Tony Robbins*

Giving can be using your time or money to make a difference to your partner, children, community, country, the planet, or the universe. Contribution can also be your legacy. Valuable contribution can be to just help one other person — it doesn't need to change the world.

Your need for Contribution has a direct relationship to having a Purpose, which is why it one of the variables in our Purpose Formula. If nobody relies on you, or if you don't provide value to anybody, then you serve very little purpose…and you will feel like it too.

Contributing does not always mean charitable work. You can also get paid for contributing. Everyone who is employed is contributing already – they provide value to customers and receive payment in return.

There is also a negative side to contribution — if you contribute too much.

For example, I met a woman on the verge of going bankrupt — which would leave her and her daughter homeless. She'd put off looking through her bank statement and her monthly expenses were out of control. One of the things she loved to do was contribute. When I checked her bank statement, I found hundreds of pounds going out to multiple charities every month. While I applauded her charitable nature, sometimes it can be to the detriment of your loved ones.

You might physically contribute so much that it negatively impacts your health, when you put other's needs so far above yours. As they advise on airplane flights — you should always put on your oxygen mask first, before helping others.

Workbook Question 28. List the main ways you achieve Contribution in your life. Positive and negative.

HOW THE 6 HUMAN NEEDS FIT TOGETHER

It's important to see which needs you focus on the most and whether you achieve them in healthy ways. Your needs shape your emotions, life, and ultimately your destiny.

If Certainty is your top need, then it can lead to a frustrating life. I was a perfectionist for many years, did very detailed planning and tried to control most things. It's IMPOSSIBLE to control everything, so it always leads to disappointment. I've since learned to let go more, to believe that things will work out, and that things can be 'good enough'.

The last three Human Needs of Love and Connection, Growth and Contribution, feed the soul. They provide you with the greatest fulfilment in life.

We learned this the hard way. When Sarah and I achieved financial freedom and quit our jobs, we spent two years thoroughly enjoying ourselves. We maintained our property empire at the same level, and our life remained static. We should have been at the peak of happiness, but we felt like there was something missing from our lives, and we couldn't put our finger on it.

Then we discovered the 6 Human Needs and it all became clear. Firstly, we'd stopped growing. We weren't buying more properties, and we weren't pushing our boundaries. Consequently, we set ourselves big goals and decided to go on courses every year, covering all areas of our life. We love reading, so we switched from fiction, to mostly non-fiction books that we can learn from and apply.

Secondly, we weren't contributing in a way that made us feel fulfilled. We had tried a number of ways. We'd regularly donated money and volunteered for multiple charities for decades. Sarah joined the PTA at school and ran the local Beavers. But nothing we did gave us a fuzzy warm feeling inside.

We discovered we most enjoyed seeing the direct impact of our contribution, rather than just paying money into a charity and not seeing the end result.

THE 6 HUMAN NEEDS AND CONTRIBUTION

We started mentoring people completely by accident. A property company asked us to mentor their students. I'd previously fantasised about becoming a teacher when I retired, so I thought, why not give it a try.

We were surprised by how good it made us feel. It bought us so much joy to watch the students' progress, and help change their lives. But we wanted deeper relationships with the mentees, and more flexibility, to fit with our lifestyle — so we after a while we left and mentored students ourselves. This act of Contribution — the final variable in the Purpose Formula, brought us fulfilment.

As Tony Robbins says, *"While the 6 human needs are deep-seated, remember that your past is not your future unless you live there. You can choose to fulfil your needs in a healthy way."*

Once you discover your purpose, you will see that it not only includes 'Contribution', but it hits many of your human needs.

Workbook Question 29. What are the top 3 human needs, you have been valuing and focusing on the most? In order of priority.

Workbook Question 30. What are the positive and negative consequences of valuing them, in that order?

Workbook Question 31. What will your top 3 human needs require to be, in order to transform your life?

How would your life improve? What will you do to replace your negative behaviours with positive ones?

For a happy and fulfilling life, I'd recommend you include at least one or more of the needs of the soul, which are Love and Connection, Growth and Contribution.

CHAPTER 11

The Purpose Formula in Action

YOUR ELEMENTS OF THE PURPOSE FORMULA

In this chapter, I'll show you how Sarah and I, plus many others, have unknowingly applied the Purpose Formula to their lives.

Passions x Gift(s) x Environment x Contribution = Purpose

What you've learned so far…

As you filled out your workbook, you identified your Life Challenges and how they may have created your Passions.

You've discovered the special Gifts you have, which are your own unique tools.

You learned how the changing external and internal Environment affect your purpose and could change it at any time.

You know how your Driving Question, Identity and Human Needs, affect the decisions you make every day.

You will probably have many different Purposes or Dharma over your lifetime.

TAKE A MOMENT TO REFLECT

Please take a moment to read and reflect upon your answers in the workbook, before reading further.

That information, together with the stories in this chapter, may give you the 'aha' moment that sparks your purpose.

THREE FEET FROM GOLD

Napoleon Hill wrote about the story of R. U. Darby and his uncle, who went digging for gold in Colorado. After a few weeks of labour, then found some ore. But they didn't have the money to mine it. So, they covered it up and went to his home in Maryland, to raise funds from his relatives and neighbours. Then they went back to mine, to dig.

THE PURPOSE FORMULA IN ACTION

They mined their first car of ore and it was really good quality. A few more carloads and they could clear their debts, then rake in their fortune.

Suddenly the vein of gold ore disappeared! They kept drilling and drilling, but they couldn't find any more. It was all for nothing.

Finally, they quit.

They sold the machinery to a junk man for a few hundred dollars and went back home.

The junk man was smarter than they thought. He called in an engineer, who made some fault line calculations, and identified that the vein should be just three feet from where the Darby's had stopped drilling.

The junk man started mining in the new spot, and found the hidden gold ore. He made millions of dollars.

Just like the story, many of us are already living, or are just three feet away from our purpose. With just a slight tweak in the direction you're heading, you can hit gold.

My current Purpose is to "Live my dream life, and help my family and others to do the same."

I didn't realise that was my purpose. But, just like the three feet from gold story, I was so close to it.

It's blindingly obvious now. I've spent my entire life using my Gifts of Technology, plus Optimising and Simplifying everything I do. Curiously, I was unaware that my Optimising was a Gift until Sarah pointed it out…so make sure you ask someone close to you about your Gifts.

I applied those Gifts to my Passions of investing, money, health, fitness, relationships, etc.

My internal and external Environment determined the focus of my energy, which led to my Purpose at different points in my life.

If you were a fly on the wall, you'd notice that I'm always tweaking all aspects of my life, to make it the best it can possibly be (Designing my Dream Life). I also do the same for my family. When I'm with my friends, I try to help them design their life too.

Most often, this revolves around becoming financially free and spending your days doing whatever brings you the most joy and fulfilment.

Passions x Gift(s) x Environment x Contribution = Purpose

Until I'd put together the formula and looked through my own life, I hadn't realised I was already living my Purpose. The problem was, I needed to recognise it, and reframe it in my mind. It now steers what I choose to do.

One way of knowing whether you are already living your purpose, is how you feel at the beginning of the week. Do you get Monday morning blues…or are you looking forward to going to work? Do you get in your element at work and feel really energised when you're there? If so, then you are most likely already living your purpose. You could use the Purpose Formula to identify which aspects of your job light you up the most, and whether you could change your responsibilities a little to make it even more fulfilling.

ENVIRONMENTAL CHANGES

Environment is the wild card in the Purpose Formula. Sometimes, the Environment throws a spanner into your life, and your Purpose changes in an instant. It can completely trump all the other variables.

When I went into massive depression and subsequently left my corporate job — I decided my only Purpose was to "Become Financially Free as fast as possible — for my family."

Looking back, I can now see I was applying my Gifts to this cause. Making money was always in my Passions. And now I had a sense of urgency due to not having a job (Environment). Finally, when Sarah was 39 years old, we achieved Financial Freedom.

For an earlier example in my life…when I was a teenager, I was overweight, short, and got bullied at school — this was both influences of the internal and external Environment.

I decided that getting bigger muscles would stop people picking on me.

It became my single Purpose. I read everything I could find on bodybuilding. Arnold Schwarzenegger became my hero. I used my Gifts to optimise my diet, supplements, exercise, sleep, everything you could think of. My entire life outside of school revolved around getting bigger. And it worked. Two years later, I was more muscular than most of the boys in my class, and the bullying stopped.

*****

An example, from Sarah — she had a lot of difficulties becoming pregnant (internal Environment). She got increasingly more and more upset, every time her period came. Having children was something she'd always dreamed of. She thought it would 'just happen.'

She spent all of her time reading books on getting pregnant, adding supplements, timing her ovulations, buying boxes of pregnancy test kits, and much more. She used her Gift of being a Scientist. Her Purpose had shifted to "Becoming a Mother."

Sarah had multiple medical investigations and interventions over the following years. Each one briefly raising her hopes and then smashing her self-worth to the ground. People all around her seemed to be getting pregnant the first month they tried, or found out they were accidentally pregnant. Walking around seeing pregnant women or mothers with new-born babies became distressing. It got more and more difficult to keep the faith that we would ever have children.

Sarah was determined to have children, whatever it took and no matter how awful the process might be. All in all, it was six years of heart-breaking emotions, before we finally had a child.

If she hadn't shifted her purpose to "Becoming a Mother," she wouldn't have had the focus and energy necessary to keep persisting when challenges arose. She also wouldn't have been able to hold the faith that it would happen, when the time was right.

Don't Deny Your Purpose

When my late father was diagnosed with type II diabetes, he retired from his job as a Senior Charge Nurse at a local hospital. With his identity and purpose gone, he drifted along in life. He soon developed Parkinson's disease. It began with noticeable tremors on one of his hands, and eventually led to loss of nearly all strength in his body and he had difficulty speaking.

My father lived in complete denial of his condition. Rather than accepting and embracing it, so he could fine tune his new purpose, he just kept telling me when he was better he would do this…when he could walk better he would do that…when he was strong enough to get out of his wheelchair he would fly to his homeland of Hong Kong. He never made that trip.

The last time I saw him properly lucid, we'd just eaten a meal in a restaurant. I pushed him outside in his wheelchair, while my mother was inside paying the bill. While standing there, he talked to me very quietly and slowly. The last thing he said to me was, *"What is your plan?"*

It was such an open question, that I didn't know how to answer him. I had no idea what my purpose was at that time. But if you're watching over me Dad, then rest in peace that I've discovered it.

Moreover, I've had a couple of different health scares myself. And I know my Purpose would have changed if any of them had become serious. If my father had set himself a Purpose focusing on his Parkinson's, his later years might have turned out differently. Perhaps, something on the lines of: *"My Purpose is to live the best life for me and my family, with Parkinson's."*

CRITICAL FOR YOUR HEALTH

There have been multiple research studies, proving that people die shortly after retirement. And that the younger you retire, the sooner you die.

I believe a major factor behind this, is due to feeling you have no purpose anymore. Your boss isn't relying on you, your colleagues aren't relying on you, your family don't rely on you for income anymore. You don't contribute to society. You're obsolete, unnecessary.

So make sure you create a purpose for yourself when you retire, or become financially free, to make sure you have a reason to get out of bed in the morning!

DRIFTING

Many people drift through life without a purpose. They just keep living the same life every day. They don't grow, or contribute. They don't wake up excited to start the day…they just 'exist.'

I see many people in retirement doing the same thing every day. Just getting from one day to the next. Many just sit in a chair all day long, and occasionally fall asleep there too.

But your purpose doesn't need to be huge, and world changing. If you have children, you could dedicate it to them and your grandchildren.

One example was a lady I met, who wanted to someday join Doctors Without Borders. She was currently going to work, day after day, with nothing to light her up. She was just putting in her time until she retired.

Her daughter had left home some time ago, so she lived alone. I asked her, "Why not rent out your home and join now?" There was really nothing to stop her from living her dream now, rather than postponing it another 15 years. Could you live your dream now?

YOUR PURPOSE CAN BE SMALL

It's okay if your purpose only helps one person, or your children. It doesn't need to be rallying the world to a single cause.

What I think is really helpful though, is to refine the wording of your purpose statement, so that it is really inspiring to you.

For example, Rose Kennedy's purpose was focused on her children. She stated her purpose as:
"My mission is to raise a family of world leaders."

She successfully raised both President John F. Kennedy, Senator Robert F. Kennedy and Senator Edward Moore Kennedy. Her daughter Jean Kennedy, was the ambassador to Ireland.

Having such a strong purpose enabled her to live to 104 years old.

Consequently, if you feel your sole purpose and reason for getting up each day, is being a mother — then think about how you can be a different kind of mother? What will be your gift to your children? How can you help them achieve to achieve their potential? How can you help them achieve independence?

Gandhi

Your beliefs become your thoughts,
Your thoughts become your words,
Your words become your actions,
Your actions become your habits,
Your habits become your values,
Your values become your destiny.
— Mahatma Gandhi

It would be difficult for me to write a book on finding your purpose, without mentioning the life of Mahatma Gandhi.

He didn't start out being respected. He was a failed barrister in India, ridiculed by his peers. Gandhi was famous for once fleeing a courtroom in terror, after being asked to present a difficult argument. After that embarrassment, no one would hire him in India.

So, at 23, he left for South Africa, to get a fresh start in his career.

It wasn't long before Gandhi started a complex legal case. His client and the opposition were relatives. He noticed that every month that went by, increased their suffering. He knew that the case would drag out for many years in the courts. It would drain the clients of money, and only enrich himself and the opposition lawyer.

But instead of lining his pocket, Gandhi convinced his client to submit the case to arbitration and settle out of court. That act eventually led to a peaceful resolution.

Gandhi said, *"My joy was boundless. I had learnt the true practice of law. I had learnt to find out the better side of human nature and to enter men's hearts. I realized that the true function of a lawyer was to unite parties riven asunder."*

Gandhi later noticed the suffering Indian community in South Africa, and became determined to live his purpose — to "unite parties riven asunder."

Gandhi created a movement, underpinned by nonviolence. He often received physical beatings, and refused to retaliate. After six years, the South African President signed a pact that led to the "Indian Relief Bill," giving Indians civil rights.

After becoming a hero in South Africa, he left for his homeland of India. His aim was to free the people from British rule and to unite the people of India. He did drive out the British. But his dream of uniting the different religions in India, ended in dividing the country.

Despite this, Gandhi is revered as a living a life of selfless, non-violent, devotion to civil rights.

But what led to Gandhi's transformation, from failed lawyer to the leader of an inspiring movement? Gandhi put it down to his devotion to the principles in the

THE PURPOSE FORMULA IN ACTION

Bhagavad Gita. He studied it constantly. He memorised it and chanted it.

Gandhi applied the Purpose Formula by using his:

Passion to live the teachings in the Bhagavad Gita
x Gifts of reconciliation and the law
x Environment of Indian inequality
x Contribution to provide selfless service to all Indians
= Purpose to "unite parties riven asunder" using non-violent actions.

CHAPTER 12

Finding and Getting Paid for Your Purpose

*"If you bring forth what is within you, what you bring forth will save you.
If you do not bring forth what is within you, what you do not bring forth will destroy you."*
— *Gospel of Thomas*

THE PURPOSE POSTER

It's your duty to live your purpose, otherwise you'll live an unfulfilling and unhappy life, and share that misery with the people around you.

Now it's time to pull it all together.

**Exercise — read through all the answers you wrote in your workbook, and fill out the Purpose Poster you downloaded:
https://rebrand.ly/purposeworkbook**

Your Purpose Poster is a concise, one-page snapshot of the key points you've written in your workbook. It's useful to put it up somewhere you can see it every day, or use it as your screensaver.

Not only does the poster make sure you are heading in the right direction on a daily basis, but is also useful to sense check new opportunities. When a new opportunity comes along, ask yourself whether it aligns with your Passions, Gifts, Ultimate Life Vision and goals.

Your poster doesn't need to be perfect. It's a work in progress and you can continue to tweak it over time. If you have any elements that you haven't decided yet, then write something rough as a guideline. That's okay.

Your purpose statement should be reasonably short and EASY for YOU to remember. It's the same advice for your Identity.

Your purpose should go beyond you — to help your loved ones, or your community, or country, or planet. That will help you to reach a higher level of fulfilment.

LIVE YOUR TRUE LIFE

"I wish I'd had the courage to live a life true to myself, not the life others expected of me."
— Bronnie Ware

Are you living someone else's purpose out of duty?

I have a wealthy doctor friend who runs a private clinic. He held all his hopes that his eldest son would become a doctor, so his son could take over the clinic when he retired. Unfortunately, his son did not get good enough grades, which was of great disappointment to his father. Fortunately, his daughter was smart enough and qualified as a doctor. Now she has the pressure and feels it's her duty to take over the family business. But is that her purpose? Will it provide her with the greatest fulfilment and joy in her lifetime? Only she can truly know.

So, I implore you. Whatever purpose you decide on, make sure it's your purpose, not someone else's. Or as Joseph Campbell says in the hero's journey — follow your bliss.

GET PAID FOR YOUR PURPOSE

As Dr John Demartini says, *"What is it that I would absolutely love to do, and how do I get handsomely paid to do it?"*

If you are serving and providing value to others, then it is only correct that there is fair exchange. It's also one of the spiritual laws: "The Law of Compensation."

Perhaps you absolutely love children. You enjoy their fascinating way of looking at the world. You love being able to play with them and act like a kid yourself. But your children have grown up and left home, and you really miss those days. Maybe becoming a childminder, or a nanny is something you'd love to do every day?

Or perhaps you love all kinds of dogs. Whenever you pass a dog, you always greet the owner and see whether you can stroke their dog. You have a dog of your own, and love spending most of your spare time playing with it. You've found it difficult to get good a sitter when you go on holiday. Consequently, you decide to start up a dog sitting service, so you can regularly spend time playing with more dogs.

When we became financially free through property investing, we had a huge amount of free time on our hands. But we felt unfulfilled. We had no purpose, and we weren't contributing in a way that resonated with us.

So, we decided to have direct contact with people, by helping people to become financially free as fast as possible, and live their true purpose, to give back to the world.

We feel so energised by this. But we knew we needed to be fairly compensated. If we trained people for free, then firstly, we would not feel obligated to turn up; and secondly, they would not get a comprehensive and structured program. Their results would be poor. We would eventually resent doing it, and decide to stop helping people.

On the student side, both ourselves and others have experienced that when you get something for free, you don't make much of a transformation. It seems not to have as much value in your mind. You don't commit fully, as you don't feel like it's any great loss to you financially, if you don't apply yourself.

Moreover, how much would it be worth to someone if you made them financially free within the next two, to five years, so they could spend a lifetime doing what they want instead? Therefore, it's important for both you and them, that you receive fair exchange for the value you provide. What is the transformation worth to people?

However, 'Fair exchange' does not always mean being paid with money, particularly if your purpose focuses on your children. In that case, your payment could be the satisfaction of building your legacy — knowing you are doing all you can to support your children and grandchildren, to create their best life.

Another example of fair exchange is having all your living costs paid for. There are plenty of jobs and volunteering opportunities where your lodging and perhaps food are provided for your labour.

As you look through your Purpose Poster, ask yourself whether there any jobs that could pull together some of those elements? The more elements the better.

Or does your current job already tick most of them off? You've been living your purpose without realising it. In which case, can you find a way to modify your job, to make it even more fulfilling? That might involve delegating some of your tasks, so you can spend more time on the things that really energise you, or you're great at.

STARTING A SIDE HUSTLE

If you can't think of an existing job that meets your purpose, then perhaps you can create your own way of getting paid for your purpose.

It's never been easier to work virtually. You can mentor people over Zoom, create digital courses, and do all kinds of office-based services from your home.

Just as a warning — starting a business is not for everyone. When you start out, you'll need to be good enough at everything, from technology, to bookkeeping, marketing, sales, and much more. Also, many people don't want the financial uncertainty involved in running your own business. I've seen many people quit their jobs to work full time on their new business…only to end up trying to get a job again.

A smarter move is to start a side hustle while you're in your current job, and to only leave when your business generates enough money. As I like to say to my students… "build your parachute, then jump."

Even an unusual combination of interests can become a viable business. Let's say you studied filmmaking at college and are really good at it (Gift). But what you really love (Passion) is cooking healthy food and working out. At first glance, you may wonder what on earth you could do for a job. However, that sounds like a health and fitness YouTuber to me, monetised by sponsorships, cookbooks, and training and diet programmes.

Alternatively, property investing is a great side hustle to do alongside your job, as it doesn't require the broad range of skills required in a regular business. But it should still be treated as a business focusing on profit, not a hobby.

We have always used investing as a tool to build wealth and create regular income, rather than being our purpose.

Our purpose is to live our dream life and help our family and others to do the same. Once you've created enough income from property, then you can quit your job, and spend time doing what you love, and would fulfil you the most.

Conclusion

All we ask is that whatever purpose you choose…don't focus on what you think will make the most money, or what your parents or others expect of you. Focus on your true purpose, and live a happy, fulfilling life.

Finally, good luck! Well done for taking the time to focus on yourself. We hope we have served you in examining and choosing your direction in life.

If you've found your new purpose – great! If you have found out that you are actually living your purpose, and embraced it fully – even better!

When Sarah went through this process, she realised that she was denying her purpose (mainly focusing on our relationship and kids), and feeling resentful of the time that she spent parenting and running the household.

Having embraced her new purpose – helping us, the kids and other people live their best lives – it gave her a new reframe on her life and has resulted in more joy and peace every day. I hope that you can achieve the same.

WE'D LOVE TO HEAR FROM YOU

Please leave a review for this book on Amazon because your review could be the one that helps someone realise that if you can find your purpose, they can take the next step to find theirs too.

If you're interested in anything we do, such as our events, training, or our vlog, please visit https://linktr.ee/sarahandgeorge

We'd feel truly blessed and inspired to see what purpose you've chosen, or any ah-ha moments you had while reading this book.

With love, Sarah & George Choy

Printed in Great Britain
by Amazon